Acknowled

Many thanks to all the friends and
continuing support; too numer
Suffice to say, you know who you are.

Special thanks to Samantha Reynolds for allowing me to use her poetry in this collection.
As always, its a pleasure.

Notes

All the content contained within this edition are original works by the author, with
notable exceptions listed in the Credits.

Credits

'Winter Strikes', 'The Reliable Sun', 'Thaw' and 'What Lies Beneath'
are original works by the author, which originally featured in the photo-poetry books
'Winter Dreams' and 'Winter Dreams 2'.

'Winter Solstice' and 'I Am The North' are original works by Samantha Reynolds, and
were originally featured in the photo-poetry book 'Winter Dreams 2'.

'Ely Cathedral' is re-worked poem by the author, which originally featured in a different
format, in a photo-poetry series by MoGeoPhotographic

'Footsteps in the Snow (Revised)' is a re-worked poem which originally featured in
'Winter Dreams 2'

"Perceptions"

A Poetry Collection

by

Ange Chan

with guest poet
Samantha Reynolds

To Cath
Enjoy!
much love
Ange Chan
x

TABLE OF CONTENTS

SEASONAL POETRY

"Perceptions"

Roses

Plant a rose to remind me of you
To remind me of everything that we've been through

A gentle pace, a memorable place
My wooden legacy marks an open space

Nostalgia's the name, but as you can see
Nostalgia ain't everything it used to be....

Forever Remembered
(A Friend's Promise)

Come with me
Come take my hand
and I will take you to a peaceful land
A place where friendship's seeds are sown
A place where sorrow is never shown
And all that is, is here and now
No tears of sadness, no furrowed brow
Just trust in me because I care
Just take my hand, and I'll be there

The Journeys End
(In memorium of Peter Reynolds, RIP)

Today has come;
The journey's end
The weeks of pain are gone
And better times now, my friend

The vultures may swirl
But they'll never find
the love that comes
With true peace of mind

I walked the path
And I'll walk once more
A thousand times over
'Til you hurt no more

So be kind to yourself
And grieve, like you must
True colours are shown
From those that we trust

Death's dark veil
Has shackled its shroud
And sunnier days
Will brighten the clouds

The passing of time
Will tick 'cross the years
Emotions will come
And so will the tears

So be kind to yourself
And do what's right
The love is always there;
Never give up the fight.

Time

Where oh where does the time go?
The clock ticks faster,
You just go with the flow.
The moments pass,
Consigned quickly to "the past"
And the memory will stay or will go.
So make moments count,
Turn those minutes into meaningful memories,
And live your life,
without the clock watching.

Regrets of the Dying

It's the end of my life, and what have I learned?
Did I toil too much, and leave my family spurned?
Did I say "I Love You" to those that I do?
Did I say it enough?
Did I say it to you?

Did I make enough time for fun spent with friends?
Were dreams and aspirations chased to the end?
Did I do what I love, instead of what's safe?
Was I true to myself?
Was I bold, was I brave?

Did I always speak my mind instead of resenting?
Was I the "bigger person" when conflict's presenting?
Did I do right by my kids, and raise them just so,
Did they have the childhood, that we all should know?

I wish I'd saved money for retirement
But regretting it now isn't time well spent
Did I live with an honour and courage and truth
Did I become a role model for the generation of youth?

I wish I'd not been so angry and proud
I wish I'd not locked myself in a shroud
Happiness is an option; I now know that's true
I wish the younger me, was telling that to you

So what have I learned through my lifetime of years
Life's what you make it, and there's nothing to fear
Live the life you desire, here and now, and today
Make the changes, don't regret.
Live life another day.

Kissed

All that's left is the kiss on my lips, as you turn and walk away
You kissed me firm and you kissed me true
there is no doubt of my love for you
You held me close in your embrace
You looked at me and you held my face

As lovers part, we always feel
The need of a kiss, to seal the deal
A kiss to show our true emotion
A kiss to prove our undying devotion
So as I stand at the platform side
I know our love has nowhere to hide
And as I turn and walk away
Your kiss will see me through the day

Kiss

A poem for lovers across the land

Kiss your lover before you leave,
For time will pass and you will grieve
A moment missed, in your history
May come to pass, and you will see
That all that's true, will belong to you
And how we act, binds love, with glue
So do what's right, felt from the soul
In a single heartbeat, it makes you whole

Misery Loves Company

Misery loves company, now ain't that the truth
For the beauty has gone, with the tide of your youth

Applied in the morning, with lipstick and bile
Then you spend the whole day, calling everyone "vile"

So look in the mirror, at the gleaming facade
It doesn't show "ugly", that's hiding inside

You might fool yourself, but all else can see
When the lies and nastiness, are directed with glee

You're relying on others, to carry you through
But they've seen the hate, and I'm sure you do too

Hiding behind your tablet or screen
Shows your true colours, but especially the green

Envy's not pretty, and neither is malice
And I'll be the one, to bring back the balance

For everyone tells me; Ignore, delete, block
But I care not for your insults, and the way that you mock

You think a lot of yourself, if your profile is true
But we know the truth, from the rubbish you spew

So take one last look, in that mirror frame
When alls said and done, you'll feel nothing but shame

You call me a blighter, well, maybe that's true
But things could be worse, I could be like you!

Trolls

Trolls may appoint many screen names
Hiding behind their monitors.
They can say what they like
Their opinions are vile; and
I have no time for pathetic games

One tactic in particular, really stinks
A pointless vendetta
To cover the truth;
Inadequacies for their own beliefs
Spewing their rancidness on my links

When face to face, a coward's revealed
No longer a brave
or "clever" soul
For all the hatred that they spurt
Wish: vitriol to consume them whole

Loyalty's challenged, and friendships laid bare
Persona revealed in many forms
Mutual acquaintances
Silence the hurt
By the knowledge of who they really are

Rock Star

Standing in the audience, watching you up on the stage
You move in time to the music, and the crowd go insane
You beg for their cries, you shout for their tears
But only I know, that's all that you fear
For the rock god within has left and gone home
And he's waiting for me to pick up the phone
To call and confirm that my heart's still at play
So you sit and drink whiskey 'til the cold light of day
You dare not display the secrets within
The rock god routine, is wearing quite thin
You lie to the fans with the charade that you bring
But they're fooled by the act through the songs that you sing
And when you leave stage for your final encore
Your heart's at my feet, and still you want more
You return to the stage where X marks the spot
And give it your all crying "now that's your lot"
Sated and spent, you go to your room
And there I am waiting in the depths of the gloom
You hold me to you, and hurt all subsides
Then locking the door we two only, inside
Removing your clothes that are sweaty and stained
You give me your love and remove all the pain
A public performance takes all of your soul
But I am with you and you make me whole
The groupies are gathering, knocking down your door
The pressure is rising; you slump to the floor
We cling into each other and block out the noise
And try to ignore cries of girls and boys
An hour has passed and gone are the fans
You gather your thoughts then reach for my hands
Alone home we go, just us two now
And back is the man that gave me his vow

You

You're braver than you think you are
When you're driving in the dark, in the rain, in your car
Emotional thoughts are cast to one side
And you lock all your doors, to stay safe within, inside

You're more talented than you are when you stand on the stage
And the audience is reacting to the ways you behave
Laughter, or silence, you hold them in your palm
When to feel excited, and when to feel calm

You're more human than you know, in front of that screen
Telling strangers who you are and where you've been
But remember it's reality reflected back at you
In the cold light of day, did you tell what's true?

You're more alive than you realise when you're sitting here with me
Putting the world to rights, talking 'bout what's on TV
Cementing my soul with friendship and love
A real lifesaver, a trouper, a peace dove

Skeletons

For Ali Jackson

Another skeleton has fallen from your past
Wrecking your present, the shadows are cast
Dark echoes mock and we'd rather forget
It's marking the future with the tinge of regret

We all have our baggage; it's how it is carried
Do you hide it away with the shame that is sullied
Or wear it on your chest like a big badge of pride
Do you have the full set, or are you denied?

Ex-lovers, wives, husbands we try to pretend
Never existed, and they weren't even friends
But fate comes a-knocking when it's least welcome
A karmic reminder of where you've come from

So shut closed that closet and all that's within
With mistakes that we made, and the wages of sin
Get on with your life; they never existed
For sanity's sake, they must be resisted

The Unicorn
For Paul Masters

Somewhere over the rainbow
In a land that's filled with truth
Lives a mythical creature
That bestows the tide of youth

It's horse-like at first glance
But has that certain glow
And it poses with a stance
That only unicorns know

Its coat a glossy white
And its tail is rainbow colours
If you should see this creature
Don't mistake it for the others

For the unicorn is rare
In all it has to behold
It glitters with a sheen
That is rarer than any gold

So cling on to the memory
When you see a unicorn
And wish upon a star;
Your life will be reborn!

Laundry
(If Kate Bush can write about it, then so can I)

How do you hang the washing out, in the midday sun?
Do you split the the darks and whites so the colours never run?

Do you even hang your clothes out under sunny sky
or shove it in the tumble, waiting for it to dry

Are you methodical or messy in your laundry routine?
You don't care how it's done, you just want everything clean!

Are the socks and smalls and undies kept separate to wash
Or does it all just get shoved in? Bish! Bash! Bosh!

Each person has their own way of getting their clothes clean
Thank God it's not by labour, you just put it in a machine

Select the programme. Add the powder and conditioner too
Which temperature to choose? Which one will get out that goo?

You sometimes watch the clothes as they tumble in the drum
Round and round hypnotically, to the "washing machine hum"

The water swishes and gurgles and Magic has its play
There's too many things to consider, when its laundry day

Is the weather good enough for me to hang a load outside?
Do you panic and get in a blether,
when you check the forecast weather?
Wondering how you'll get it all dry
As you look up at rainy skies

Kismet 2

When the stars are aligned it's obvious to see
That these love emotions, were meant for just you and me

You liberate my soul into something that's true
And the love that we share is meant for us two

Its written in the galaxy, no one can deny
And the horoscopes that tell our fate, are nothing but a lie

We've even been in, the same room before
but fate played it's hand to even the score

With the passing of time, the stars are aligned
A mutual attraction, in this time, is forged

Fragmented souls join as one
A lifetime of hearts bonded, has just begin

The seal of love's approval is not required here
for chemistry and magic are at play, and there is nothing to fear

There's no one else to challenge when sparks that true attraction
The heart beats faster, eyes dilate; a cosmic chemical reaction

A Quick Lesson of How to Use Facebook

Facebook is the place to be
For posting photos of your tea
For moaning online when no-one cares
And when you're ill or have fallen down stairs
It's great for posting all those selfies
Or even cartoons of "self-as-elfies"
So many birthday wishes to make
And adding piccies of your cake
For playing games like "Candy Crush"
Or status updates when you're in a rush
They give a snapshot of your life
Your kids, your house, your cat, your wife
Funny meme's may make you laugh
Just don't post photos whilst in the bath!
Topical jokes, and hating the Tories
Telling lies and making up stories
Books you've read, and photos of cats
Whinges, moans and nasty spats
Hateful comments make it there too
Just hope and pray that they're not about you!
Song lyrics which tug at your heart
Or remind you of a time when you were torn apart
Its a place to make a difference
Or changing views of your friends, your audience
For hating Cancer and other diseases
Or telling the world when your kid has the measles
Videos of songs that you really love
For poking people (or giving a shove)
Yes Facebook is the place to be
And especially great for poets like me!

Twitteratti

Observing life
One hundred and forty characters
at a time
A soundbite for an emotion,
Thought or deed
Follow
Unfollow
RT
Block/Delete
For thoughtless words
From total strangers

View into the spyhole of my life
And form an opinion
based on a short sentence
Come, observe
Judge

There are no "likes" here
Be a friend
Form a group
Of like minded souls
With similar interests

Friends from countries a far
Time zones shattered
Through the complicity
Of duplicity

So give me a minute or three
To interact with strangers on my PC
Internet friends
Who are stranger than me
Avoiding the rubbish
On my TV

Ely Cathedral

On the last day of my fortieth year
I stepped in your shadows.
I drank in your mystery,
Your knaves, and your majesty.

Laid
So many years before me,
And will lay
So many years after

I have diminished.

The secrets in your stonework
The bodies, entombed.
Medieval mysteries,
Stories, taken to the grave

Liaisons 'twixt two persons
that will never behold
Dark mysteries
Witnessed
Never to be told
Perpetual lies
of a magnitude so rare
And a grandeur of presence,
So bold.

Hangover

With my head held in my hands
I'm paying for my sins
A late night of fun with friends
And this is how it ends

I know the script by now
Having suffered many times
Yet still I willingly return to the scene
of my perpetual crimes

Reluctantly accepting the consequence
I'm not your commodity
what I always do doesn't make much sense
So please don't compromise my modesty

Bluebells

There's nothing more charming
than a bluebell wood.
Just sit there for a while,
and tell me....
don't
you
feel
good?

Life is affirmed
Your troubles will fade
And memories of youth' s past
Plays out,
in an azure glade

Pure positivity rings out
from those mini bells
Delivering their charm
And the love that they tell

The faeries carry their magic
On their wings
and the breeze
So sit
awhile
Let life pass you
Smell their intoxication

Be calm

Feel good

The Cool Side of the Pillow

The cool side of the pillow
Is where I like to lie
It brings me peace in slumbers
Its how I want to die

For on that side of the pillow
Good dreams will surely flow;
The other side's for nightmares
An a life I don't want to know

So show me the stuff that dreams are made of
Of lovers and places and fun
Give me the cool side of the pillow
And a lifetime of dreaming's begun

Frances

Silk Cut fags and lavender soap
Max Factor face powder, thickly applied
Stories of wartime rationing,
peppered liberally with a side of lies

Trinkets stuffed in a drawers,
forgotten gifts of love
Untangled, just for play
My childhood self, easily pleased

Two bathrooms, there's posh
Izal loo paper; makeshift kazoo's
A proper pantry and industrial packets
Tom & Jerry stickers on the twin tub

Me, 8 years old, and buying fags by the carton
from the "offy" to keep her supplies in check
Sneaky sweets bought with the change
A payment in kind for chores delivered

Open heart surgery; more attacks than Hiroshima
Bungalow living, and ghosts in the hallway.
Library room stuffed with books never read
Strange noises heard as I lie on the Z-bed

Swirly patterned carpets, in brown and orange
Fake Rococo wardrobes, gold paint detail by my Mum
Cigarettes on the go in every room
Smog hanging, worse than LA at dawn

Field opposite full of horses, fed peelings and waste,
A childhood duty, I was terrified.
Pothole road unadopted, just like kids
Bypass views of cars whizzing by

Red Mini clubman that went like the clappers
Moving to Scotland just for kicks
Nostalgia ain't what it used to be….
Blackpool care home, depressing as sin

Three weddings, but only one real marriage
Brandy and pills cocktail,
and false phone conversations from afar
Emergency dashes and lifts from the station

Smart red suit with red velvet collar
Promises made, and duly unkept.
Green glass ornaments with white painted snowdrops
Arabesque Denby, Puffin duvets, Staying over for weeks

Alice's Last Stand

Climbing to the summit
Of self appointed gloom
My feather-like touch
Will topple your mountain
There will be no salvation in the truth
And rocks will fall
Like tears spilling from my jar
You pierce my red heart
With your words of stone
Emotionless and hard and jagged
My eagle will
Swoop and circle
Protecting my soul
From your vulturesque words
Raining down like lava
Melting and destroying
All in it's path

You fall down the rabbit hole of solitude
And I remain strong
At the cave's mouth of discontent
Fighting off all
Who threaten my brood
With all the strength
And patience of the Jabberwokky
Poised to attack
Yet choosing its precise moment
To disappear in a
Magician's plume of smoke.

My deep red heart will fall apart
Like a house of cards,
Tumbling down, down, down
Into a room of decisions
Drink, eat, or despair

Looking through the glass
Into the garden of delights
When regal promises
Of wanton acts of destruction
Are dispensed in a heartbeat
And memories of tea and cakes
And smoking insects
Are the pathway home
From your dreams
Marking the crumbs of reality
Home....
To your waking state.

Disenfranchised

Chained to the memory of you.
A lifetime has passed
Its now time to forget....
But your deceit taints my future
My trusting element defiled
No matter how I try
My emotions are defeated
Surrendered to duplicity
By a silence so strong
My conclusions are drawn
Be they right or wrong.
Dead memories fill my heart
When my world imploded
But jigsaw times were had
Dancing outside of the shadows
But then, destroying my soul and
Put back on the shelf.
Since then, I found myself.
Oh, the hearts that you break
The lies beneath truth
And reality, opaque.

Forging my tight family ties
So that nothing can pervade.
Protecting my child from alien antics
By shrouding him in love's cloak.
My fortress of invisibility,
So impenetrable
We only destroy from within.
Moving to the sequence of seven
In a metronomic daze
Better times lie in the future
At last! The life I should live,
You took away everything,
But there's so much more to give.

Vengeance

Revenge is a dish that is best served chilled
when it's not quite so hard and venom-filled

Marinate those feelings of anger and pain
Then deliver with relish along with the main

The deceit and the lies that you have told
will come back to you, 100-fold

Karma's a bitch, you know that is true
But it's only a bitch, when you are too

So watch behind you if you've got something to hide
Before life kicks you up the backside

For vengeance will come to those that believe
My feelings are clear and my hearts on my sleeve

I have not forgotten and I won't forgive
When you tried to destroy the words that I give

But just like a Phoenix from ashes, I rise
And karma will come, to deliver the surprise

I'm Every Woman

I'm Keira Knightly pretty
I'm Angelina slim
I'm Lindsay Logan shitty
I'm Alexis on a whim

I'm Debbie Harry savvy
A New York talkin' dame
I'm Mama Cass heavy
When I'm not playin' the game

I'm Joan Rivers funny
I'm Collins greatest fan
I'm Sandra Bullock sunny
And I'm every woman

I'm Julia Roberts happy
I'm Marilyn's biggest threat
I'm often Streisand sappy
I'm Bassey for a bet

I'm Siouxsie in my soul
Some things will never change
I'm all of the above
But most of all, I'm Ange

I'm Pavlova's greatest dance
I'm Ella Fitzgerald's soul
I'm Audrey Hepburn elegance
I'm many parts of the whole

I'm Jane Russell sexy
I'm Betty Davis bold
I'm Mae West flippin' foxy
I'm a pleasure to behold

"My Cities"

Barcelona

Catalonian casa, of gaudy Gaudi art
No corners or sharp edges
hinder your feng shui paradise
A paradigm of design
Sings to my soul
And takes me to its heart

Strolling down Las Ramblas
or exploring the Gothic Quarter
I feel my life lived here in another life
In this Spanish city, so rare
Its streets sing to me
Every Rincón, a symphony of sounds

And your cuisine tantilises my taste
Both seaside shanties and gothic antics
Appeal to my Gemini soul

Never change, oh Barcelona!

Note: The Spanish word Rincón is translated into "nooks and crannies"

London

As I walk o'er Blackfriars Bridge
I contemplate the Thames;
The tide is out,
And pebbled shores
Reveal the treasure
Once concealed beneath the waves.
Their watery blanket
Shielding them from the grey clouds
Forming patterns in the sky.

I view the vista before me
of trains and boats and cars, and
Cyclists, on their borrowed bikes
Tube trains felt under-foot,
Their rumblings below my shoes
Almost as loud as my hunger.
For this city
A rhythmic metronome for the metropolis
A pulsating beat
An ever-changing landscape...

I shall return tomorrow
And I will not recognise my scene
For this cannot be preserved.
London's chameleon skin will have morphed
Into something unrecognisable
from the here and now.
Grey skies may disappear
Revealing the smirking sun
Cocky, in its reverie.
Or damp pavements
littered with disgruntled commuters
Hurrying towards their vocations.
Such are London's streets; unique
Yet oblique.

Monochrome Manhattan Metropolis

In the Fall of '98
Your streets provided my sanctuary
I ran to you, to protect me,
from myself
To discover me,
myself
When my life was shattered
By love's aggressor.

I stood in wonderment at your shores
The sea and surf , of
Hudson's great moat
Protecting your turrets and castlements
Where I resided
Within monochrome walls
of Manhattan's mystery

Contemplating my future
Unaware, as I was
That's life's path, would
lead me to you again and again
Would bring your people
to my heart
Would caress my ears
with their songs of joys and misery
Would bless my heart
with their love and empathy
Would heal my soul
with a new view of the world

And so,
You are part of me
My monochrome Manhattan metropolis,
And long may it
be

Amsterdam

Your streets are as familiar to me
As your network of Canals
Are tears to me.
I have walked your paths
In recent years
More times than I can remember
Happy times associated
A litmus test of relationships
Hate what you are;
Hate what I am
For you are me, and I am you

Forget the sycophantic view
Even the tourist view
of tulips, sex and frites.
To me you are unique.
As I sit in your cafes
Familiar and comfortable as an old clog.
Your currency has changed
Over the years
But your soul has
always remained true

I walk your streets alone,
At midnight
And feel no fear of crime.
The only crime in my heart, being
That you will leave me
And my memory of who you are.

Ode to Liverpool

Port of Northwest's heart.
Eternal gateway.
Delivered me love and friendship
Over the years.
A history so rich to my country's age,
And the history of my past.
The city of culture with
Heart as big and
Soul twice as deep
As the Mersey.
Re-birthed in recent times
To a place of lambananas and magic.
Super cool location
And of much to be proud.
When I'm within you,
I'm an honorary Scouser,
Held to it's bosom
Like a mother to a child.
Home from home
I return to you and
Familiarity does not breed contempt.
Your contemporary facade protects the history
Inherent within.
The unique beating heart
Of this city of cities.
Divided by shirts of red and blue
United in grief and justice.

JFT96

Manchester, Oh Manchester

When I look to the grey skies
Full of rain and ire
I think of you
Precipitating on my parade
since puberty....
Walking your streets, with mates
A million miles or more
You've seen my stiletto spikes, pumps and heels
to your pavements
And borne witness to my happiness,
and tears
Friendships forged
To be lost and found
Memories beyond compare
And the home
to so much musical legacy
and the much missed "Mr Manchester"
Who made history
Not money
Brought life to souls
And fostered a dancing spirit
To a generation
Perfect party people.
A legacy so deserved and true
The city still mourns the loss of you
Gone too soon with no natural successor
Save a legion of legacies which live on
Through the music you facilitated

Manchester, oh Manchester
So much to answer for
From The Smiths to The Hollies
From Bee Gees to New Order
Generational genius

Seasonal Poetry

Winter Strikes

On a Hallowe'en dawn
Lights Scorpio sun, and,
Brings the frost of tomorrow
On a pale zephyr wind,
Whispering, quietly
"Jack Frost is a-comin'"...
You hear it on the breeze,
Dancing,
Through the trees.
It's branches steadfast
despite Winter's breath
Pervading,
Removing leaves,
Caressing
Forming an auburn path of rust and hues
That will turn to mush by the end of the day

Dusk arrives.

Too quickly.

The day is not done
but natures closed sign is deftly displayed.
Unwritten invitation for Jack Frosts' arrival
To place his magic touch on Earth's crust
And lay his hands to leave an icy crepe
On all that remains still
For many moons, til Aquarius acquiesces.

Thaw

As winter wends its weary way,
Toward more Spring-like days,
Consider the beauty of nature's frosty haze,
And icy sheets of purest glaze.
The Magician in Mother Nature,
Turning mere water
Into mystical forms,
And snowy blankets
Covering the truth that lies beneath.
Momentarily,
Reality is blurred... And nature's icy veil
Presents an illusion on the grandest scale,
Until the certainty of the thaw in later days.
All trees equal in the snow,
Ash, Oak, Yew, Pine.
All covered the same.
Until the thaw of their tomorrows.

Brighton Springs

Winter chills, and stinging eyes
Wrap up warm in a cosy disguise

Scarves pulled closer as wind whips features
Try to find warmth. The habits of such creatures.

Pavement walk and pebbled beach,
Prawns, cockles, ice cream?   One of each!

Spring-like days are due to come,
Though Winter remains through the watery sun.

The unwelcome freeze is weeks overdue,
and nature's confused by the lack of the dew.

Lace on the window should be lost at all costs,
Be gone gusty outbursts and wintry frosts

North Laines are bustling but seats (outside cafes) remain empty,
reflecting the chill; it's the same there in Kemp Town.

The unseasonal cold, we cannot cope
And for a warmer Spring we pray and we hope

Coughs and sneezes brought by Baltic breeze
Whilst all over Britain the rest of us freeze

Enough! Mother Nature, please nurture and bring
The warmth and optimism, only found in Spring!

Summer Solstice

Summer solstice on anniversary's eve
Awash the daylight of my youth
Penetrate the skies with warmth and colour
Pervading starry night's slumber
The dawn marked in time by a twittering chorus
And long shadows darken the solstice morn
Dew glistens in the dappled light
Sun rises high and June proudly shines
Gemini's motion so deftly remaindered
Til the cusp of Cancer's twilight

Winter Solstice
By Samantha Reynolds

Winter Solstice
The remembrance of loss
Still an icy claw around
My heart

The dead of winter but,
A time of renewal
Our road back to the light
Will start

The darkest of days
The longest of nights
And I fear that my courage
Will fail

As we wait for the world
To draw breath, to still and sigh
And gently, gently
Exhale.

The spring bulbs
That I planted for you, will waken
As the sun returns slowly to the skies
Above

Winters loss
That I carry within me
Will be tempered with the earths renewal
And a child's forever
Love.

I Am The North
By Samantha Reynolds

I, am The North
My winters touch the
Celtic heart of my
Highlands and Islands
Relentlessly
Beautifully

I, am The North
My mountains bear
Winters wet, white gift
On their northern faces
Beautifully
Relentlessly

I, am The North
My winters freeze
Landscapes and horizons
My people bear, winters caress
Relentlessly
Beautifully

In, The North
Spring arrives in my
Lowlands and cities'
Her warmth, seeps ever,
Further, northward
And, once again my
Highlands and Islands
Bloom
Beautifully
Relentlessly.

Chi mi'n geamhradh *(I see winter)*
Chi mi'n earrach *(I see spring)*
Chi mi'n am cuairt-beatha *(I see the turn of life)*

The Reliable Sun

The sun will not shine today
It will hide behind the heavy haze of the mists of winter
Frosts friend, which coats the branches with its icy touch
The heavy air thick with moisture
Waiting for the night to fall
And claim the day unto itself

The rain will not fall today
The snow will be kept away by the loss of the sun
The trees will not relent to the rainfall
The air will stay on the dry side of the precipice
And when the night falls
The moon will shine

The snow will fall tonight
The air is anticipating its duty
To freeze the fall and coat the trees with its powdery form
And when the night is ended
A new day will come
And the sun will shine

English Summer

Scorpio's precipitation
taints July's Gemini skies
No nightingale song at dawn's early light
The patter of the rain
is the anthem of the morning
Singing it's scorn for the summer of today
Tomorrow's blooms will fail
My summer's currency will outweigh the winter
And the day will end as it began

Nature's Jewels

Spider's web unbroken,
dew clinging to its wings.
Lacy strands so fragile,
With the natural beauty it brings.

It's dancing diamond strands,
Frame the tree to which it clings,
A necklace of nature's making,
Precious jewels.
Beautiful things.

What Lies Beneath

Skeletal forms, naked to the breeze,
Shadowy silhouettes, and monochrome trees

Failing wintry sun plays tricks with our eyes,
Whilst glittering confetti falls from the skies

Mesh-like brambles, now a snowy cacophony,
A single path formed by a student of photography

To capture the mood of the silent snow,
Whilst beneath its surface,
Life still grows

Footsteps in the Snow
(Revised)

Walking down the country lane
Frosted fronds greet us again,
They nod their heads in serene greeting
Their lacy strands, their beauty fleeting.

Virgin steps in snow of white
Traversing through the dappled light
Wrapped up warm in season's clothes
Rejoicing life in the winter's throes

The cold air chills my exposed face
A spider's web forms a mesh of lace
Trees mark our path of way unknown
Nature's landmarks for our way home

The snow is still as it floats to ground
An icy glaze of all that's around
Cosy coats, and hats and gloves,
Two walking figures, holding hands, in love.

Storm

Clouds are heavy in flesh toned hues
Animals ears pricked in knowing ways
Storm is travelling from distant lands
Birds of flight have stowed away
Then rain and thunder all around
Carving up the days remains
Lightning flash in strobe-like calm
Night like day, before the dawn
Crows form a group with murderous intent
Squawking their sycophantic symphony
On telegraph lines of analogue
Humidity hangs with crackling intent
Electrified oxygen, heavy on the bass
Forks of anger, electrified
Then comes the rain, of discontent

Summer Rain

Water gushing from the skies
Deluging precipitation.
Neighbour's gutters overflowed
And sodden lawns filled with clover
Rinsing away the stifling sun
And midden heat which steals your sleep
Open windows now sealed for summer
Whilst rivulets form on frosted panes.
Cleansing atmospheric hues
And bringing freshness, damp and cool
Welcomed weather in midst of heat
Despite the thunderous booming intent
No hint of blue in colourless skies
And here to stay til morning's dew

Winter Clothes

Today I'm wearing winter clothes
In tones of grey and black
Dodging raindrops and dirty puddles
Whilst utilising my raincoat and boots
Retrieved from the depths of my wardrobe
Optimistically placed for later in the calendar
August's precipitation makes way for
Sharpened pencils and pristine uniforms
For the children returning to their education
Whilst parents process their devastation…

Two days ago I was wearing a summer dress
Too warm days by the English Coast
Devouring fish and chips, and ice cream
Expected foodstuffs of delight
The dry sand between my toes
And the smell of salt in my tangled mane.
Such recent times are hard to reconcile
When Autumn's veil shrouds the light of today
And washes my memories clean away

September's Dawn

September's dawn comes all too soon
The punctuation mark of the summer
Brings freshly sharpened pencils
And neatly pressed uniforms
Which will only survive 'til Yuletide

The leaves are still green
but will change to shades
Of autumns hues
Marking the chilly death of summer
However great our hopefulness
Russets, golds and reds
Will mark the passing of the sun
Bringing foggy days and early nights

The month of perpetual changes
in nature and in routines
The ninth month of the calendar
Is the time for renewal
Shunning the rule of seven.
A dress rehearsal for the year's end
Promises made to work smarter
Diets start losing pounds
In time for the party season
When all hard efforts
Prove to be in vain...

September's dawn comes all too soon
Never ready for the catalyst month
To transition back from butterflies
Into cocoons; cosy and warm

October's Presence

I am a Lioness of October's dawn
Defending my young with love and truth
All that is loved and lost, occurs here
The tenth day in the sequence of my month
On the edge of the mutual joining
I am your Queen and you are my King;
United in the tenth house
On the cusp of Scorpio's rising
Bringing the anniversary day
To see the month's ending
Before Hallow's Eve claims me
As it's own

About the Author

Ange Chan was born in Lancashire, and subsequently lived in South Wales and Cheshire before settling in Hertfordshire, where she currently lives with her husband Steve, and son James.   In June 2012, Ange gave up on the corporate world after 26 years, to concentrate on her writing career.

Her poetry has featured in a number of collaborative projects with photographers Peter Parkinson, and MoGeo Photographic as well as with Scottish poet, Samantha Reynolds some of which are featured in this edition.   Her previous work has been published over the past 25 years in a variety of publications and websites. In July 2013, Ange performed one of her short stories on London's Southbank stage to a paying audience.

Her first full, solo collection of poetry *"Observations"* was released on Amazon in May 2014 to positive reaction.   It's available in both Kindle and paperback editions and embodies themes of love, life, and the darker side of the emotional spectrum. This volume, *"Perceptions"* continues and develops those themes.

Contact Detials
Twitter   @angechanwriter
Facebook page   "Ange Chan Writer"
Website   http://vodkaangel22.wix.com/vodkaangel22

Guest Poet

Samantha Reynolds, Scottish poet

I have worked with Samantha in the past and found her style of poetry to be extremely thought-inducing, heartfelt and organic. I'm delighted that she has agreed to contribute some of her work to this collection and I'm privileged to call her the best of friends. When we work alongside friends sometimes the synergy doesn't flow in the same way it does in your day-to-day relationship, however this is most definitely not the case here. I experience a great deal of empathy and admiration towards Samantha's poetry and I'm proud to include it in this, my second, collection. ~ Ange

Samantha lives in Edinburgh, having moved down from the Highlands in 2006. Born into a military family, Samantha is something of a nomad and has lived here, there and indeed just about everywhere, but now calls Scotland home. Having failed specularly at school, she moved to London in her teens seeking fame and fortune in a number of artistic disciplines. For a time she tread the path of a prospective journalistic career, being published in Record Mirror and the NME. She also pursued a singing/dancing/acting career, and earned an Equity Card. However, fame and fortune were not to be, and after returning to the West of England, where her parents had settled, Samantha decamped to Scotland for once and all.

She is the mother of Elizabeth and Michael and the partner of Jeff ,and now works in a homeless hostel in the Leith area of Edinburgh. Samantha been writing poetry, in both English and Gaelic for a number of years and hopes to continue to publish now that the muse has struck.

Contact Details
Email sammyagogo@gmail.com